THE HEALING CODE...

*A CIO's and CTO's Guide to
Cost-Effective, Resilient, and AI Touched Healthcare
Product Development.*

THE HEALING CODE...

*A CIO's and CTO's Guide to
Cost-Effective, Resilient, and AI Touched Healthcare
Product Development.*

Nilesh Maheshwari

Worldwide Published by
Pendown Press

PENDOWN PRESS LLP
An ISO 9001 & ISO 14001 Certified Co.,
Regd. Office: 3767A, Kanhaiya Nagar,
Tri Nagar, Delhi-110035
Ph.: 8130886000, 9650072927
E-mail: info@pendownpress.com
Branch Office: 1A/2A, 20, Hari Sadan, Ansari Road,
Daryaganj, New Delhi-110002
Ph.: 011-45794768
Website: PendownPress.com

Edition: 2024
Price: ₹ 499/-
ISBN: 978-93-6338-577-1

All Rights Reserved
All the ideas and thoughts in this book are given by the author and he is responsible for the treatise, facts and dialogues used in this book. He is also responsible for the used pictures and the permission to use them in this book. Copyright of this book is reserved with the author. The publisher does not have any responsibility for the above-mentioned matters. No part of this publication may be reproduced, distributed, or transmitted in any form or by any means, including photocopying, recording, or other electronic or mechanical methods, without the prior written permission of the publisher and author.

Layout and Cover Designed by Pendown Graphics Team
Printed and Bound in India by Thomson Press India Ltd.

To All The Healthcare Professionals, Innovators, And Dreamers Who Are Committed To Transforming Patient Care Through Technology. Your Relentless Pursuit Of Improvement And Compassion Inspires The Advancements We Strive For In This Field. May This Work Contribute To Your Journey And Support The Evolution Of A Healthier Future For Everyone.

TABLE OF CONTENTS

Foreword 1
Acknowledgement 3
Introduction: The Software Prescription 5
Why This Book? 9
Who is This Book For? 10

PART 1
The Healthcare Landscape and Software Product Engineering 11

Chapter-1
The Need for Transformation in Healthcare............................ 14

Chapter-2
Understanding the Healthcare Ecosystem 18

Chapter-3
Software Product Engineering for Healthcare........................ 26

PART 2
Building Software Products for Healthcare: From Concept to Creation 30

Chapter-4
Defining User Needs and Requirements 32

Chapter-5
Designing User Interfaces for Healthcare Software 36

Chapter-6
Software Development Lifecycle (SDLC) for Medical Devices............ 42

PART 3
Implementing and Maintaining Healthcare Software: Navigating the Real-World Landscape 50

Chapter-7
Deployment, Integration, and Interoperability: Bringing Your Healthcare Software to Life 52

Chapter-8
Validation, Verification, and Regulatory Approval 58

Chapter-9
Maintenance, Support, and Continuous Improvement for Healthcare Software 66

PART 4
Building Software Products for Healthcare: From Concept to Creation 71

Chapter-10
Emerging Technologies in Healthcare Software: A Glimpse into the Future 73

Chapter-11
The Ethical Implications of Healthcare Software: Navigating a Responsible Path............... 79

Chapter-12
Conclusion: The Road Ahead for Transforming
Healthcare – A Call to Action 84

Appendix
A: Glossary of Healthcare Terms 87
B: Resilient Product Development Framework (RPDF) 91
C: Sample User Stories and Acceptance Criteria 98

Next Page: The Future 110

Foreword

The relentless 'beep' of a cardiac monitor was once synonymous with the boundaries of modern medicine. Now, thanks to advancements in remote monitoring, that beep echoes far beyond hospital walls – it follows patients into their homes and daily lives. As the CIO/CTO of a company at the forefront of this transformation, I've seen firsthand both the challenges and the tremendous possibilities of building products responsible for extending care and improving lives.

This book, The Healing Code, is more than just a technical guide; it's a compass. It doesn't shy away from the complexities unique to our field: the life-critical nature of our devices, the ever-present need for flawless security, and the ethical considerations that come with large-scale health data. It addresses these not as roadblocks but as fundamental pillars upon which we build trust with patients and providers alike.

From regulatory intricacies to the nuances of user-centered design for an often-older population, this book offers CIOs and CTOs the practical knowledge essential for healthcare product success. But crucially, it also emphasizes the leadership needed for this technology to reach its full potential.

Building connected healthcare products is akin to extending the reach of the human heart. It requires precise engineering, unwavering resilience, and a profound understanding that with every bit of data, we hold a life in our hands. This book is for the developers, the architects, and the visionaries committed to healing beyond the hospital room.

And to Nilesh Maheshwari – you didn't just write the code; you infused it with the pulse of humanity.

Shashi Tripathi

CEO of Sleepiz and Managing Partner at Nurture Growth Fund

❖ ❖ ❖

Acknowledgements

Dear Readers,

I am grateful for the opportunity to share my experiences and insights with you. This book is a compilation of years of experience, learning, and growth. I hope the words within these pages inspire, inform, and resonate with each of you.

I am deeply thankful to the wonderful individuals who have played instrumental roles in shaping my journey and contributing to my achievements.

My wife, Deepa, you are not just my partner but the foundation of my strength. I couldn't have done this without your love and patience.

Rishvanjay, Ankita, and Aalind, my wonderful children, your laughter and joy infuse my days with purpose and motivation. You inspire me to reach for the stars.

My team at Emorphis Technologies, you have been my support, guide, and friends. Thank you for believing in me and walking this journey with me.

My mentor, friend, guru, and brother, Akshar Yadav, your guidance and wisdom have shaped me into the person I am today. I owe much of my success to your invaluable mentorship.

I am also thankful to my friend Dinesh Verma, CEO of Pendown Press, and his team for their support and suggestions throughout the creative process.

To all those mentioned and those not named, your contributions have been crucial to my journey. Together, we have built something extraordinary, and I look forward to continuing our journey of growth and success with each one of you.

Thank you for being a part of this shared experience.

Regards

Nilesh Maheshwari

❖ ❖ ❖

Introduction: The Software Prescription

You're At the Forefront of a Revolution—Yes, You Heard It Right!

The line between medicine and technology is blurring, and as a CIO or CTO in healthcare, you're not just watching it happen—you're driving it. The software you're building isn't just ticking boxes or automating processes - it's extending the reach of care, empowering patients, and enabling clinicians to make more informed decisions than ever before.

The potential? Boundless. The challenges? Enormous. But you're up to it.

Imagine a heart patient whose implanted device seamlessly communicates with an AI-driven platform, providing early warnings that prevent a crisis. Or a clinician in a remote clinic tapping into a vast knowledge base, powered by software, to diagnose a rare condition. These aren't just possibilities; they're the future you will create.

But let's be real: The journey from vision to reality is no walk in the park Your software isn't just another product; it's a lifeline. The stakes are higher, the scrutiny sharper. When lives hang in the balance, accuracy and reliability aren't optional—they're everything. Regulatory compliance isn't just a hurdle to clear, it's a core element of design. Patient data is crucial, and security must be woven into the DNA of your software. This is where your technical mastery becomes a form of patient care.

"The Healing Code" is your blueprint for achieving this balance. We won't shy away from the intricate world of HIPAA regulations, security protocols, and the ethical dilemmas of handling healthcare data. But within that framework, you'll discover strategies to drive innovation, design for real-world clinical needs, and lead teams capable of building products as precise as they are powerful and precise products.

This book is both practical and inspirational. It recognizes that CIOs and CTOs in healthcare aren't just coding – they're collaborating with clinicians, safeguarding patient well-being, and shaping the tools that will define a healthier tomorrow. Think of this book as your toolkit for turning ideas into game-changing solutions, and eventually improved outcomes

So, are you ready? Ready to build a future where software doesn't just support healing—it is healing? A future where technology isn't just a tool, but a force that empowers both patients and providers? That future isn't on some distant horizon...

It starts right here, right now, with you!

- **The Accelerating Role of Software in Healthcare Delivery**
  - **Data is the New Diagnostic:** Emphasize the power of software to analyze massive datasets, unlocking insights impossible through traditional methods (e.g., early disease detection patterns or personalized treatment prediction).
  - **Beyond Hospital Walls:** Explore how software breaks down physical barriers through telehealth, connected devices, and patient self-management tools. Healthcare becomes continuous, not just something that happens during appointments only.
  - **Empowering Patients as Partners:** Focus on the shift from patients as passive recipients of care to active participants using software-driven tools (e.g., wearable tracking or apps for managing chronic conditions).
- **Unique Challenges of Healthcare Software vs. Other Industries**
  - **Regulatory Rigor:** View compliance as more than just a box to check—see it as a creative constraint that drives innovation. It challenges you to develop secure, interoperable solutions that always prioritize patient safety.
  - **The Ethical Equation:** A lot needs to be done regarding the handling of sensitive health data, addressing bias in algorithms used during this process, and ongoing ethical considerations required for any developments in healthcare settings.

- **Clinical Complexity:** Focus on understanding medical workflows, patient-provider interactions, and the importance of building software that enhances clinical outcomes rather than complicates processes.

➢ **Why Do CIOs and CTOs Need a Comprehensive Guide?**
- **From Tech Lead to Healthcare Leader:** Success involves fluency in medical language, navigating change management within these environments, and fostering connections between technical teams and clinical stakeholders, as emphasized in this book.
- **Balancing Innovation with Responsibility:** Innovation in healthcare is exciting, but it comes with high stakes. This book will provide you with the frameworks to prototype rapidly, iterate smartly, and keep patient care at the heart of your innovations.
- **A Bridge to the Future:** Position 'The Healing Code' as your roadmap to the future of healthcare technology. It will help you anticipate and strategically integrate emerging trends like AI, Blockchain, and IoMT into the healthcare sector, ensuring that you're not just keeping up but leading the way.

❖ ❖ ❖

Why This Book?

- **Practical, not preachy:** Real-world solutions for healthcare's toughest tech challenges.
- **Stay ahead of the curve:** Discover the latest trends and innovations shaping the industry.
- **Better patient care, better business:** Learn how to use software to improve lives and profits.

❖ ❖ ❖

Who is This Book For?

➤ **Healthcare Visionaries:** Leaders seeking a competitive edge through digital transformation.

➤ **Tech Pioneers:** Software experts ready to conquer the complexities of healthcare IT.

➤ **Change Agents:** Those passionate about improving patient outcomes through innovation.

So, what are we waiting for? Let's step into this groundbreaking journey that will illuminate new horizons and redefine our understanding.

❖ ❖ ❖

Part 1

The Healthcare Landscape and Software Product Engineering

The healthcare industry is at a crossroads. Escalating costs, the rising prevalence of chronic diseases, and aging populations are placing significant challenges on traditional healthcare delivery methods. There is a growing demand for more personalized care that is easily accessible to patients, while healthcare providers are seeking ways to work more efficiently and achieve better outcomes. In this dynamic environment, software emerges as a key driver of change, with the potential for immense transformation.

Part 1 of this book serves as the foundation for understanding how software product engineering can revolutionize healthcare. We'll embark on a journey that explores the current state of healthcare, its inherent challenges, and the exciting possibilities software holds for the future.

Here's what you can expect to discover in this section:

- **The Urgency for Transformation:** We'll examine why change in healthcare is not just optional but a necessity. With the growing burden of chronic conditions, limitations in current care models, and relentless cost pressures, the urgency for transformation is clear. By understanding these challenges, we'll uncover where software can make the most significant impact, addressing inefficiencies and driving improvements in care delivery.

- **Navigating the Healthcare Ecosystem:** Healthcare is a complex web of interconnected stakeholders. We'll introduce you to the key players, including patients, providers, payers, and regulators, and explain their roles in the overall system. Understanding the motivations and needs of each stakeholder is crucial for designing software solutions that truly address the challenges of healthcare delivery.

- **Software Product Engineering for Healthcare:** Software for healthcare isn't like software for any other industry. In this chapter will bridge the gap between traditional software development and the unique requirements of the healthcare industry. We'll explore how established methodologies like Agile and Waterfall can be adapted to fit the healthcare context. We'll also delve into user-centered design principles and design thinking, emphasizing the importance of understanding both patient and provider needs for optimal software solutions. And we won't shy away from the critical topics of usability and accessibility, ensuring that healthcare software serves everyone equitably.

By the end of Part 1, you'll be equipped with a solid understanding of the healthcare landscape and a clear vision of how software product engineering can play a pivotal role in its transformation. You'll be prepared to dive deeper into the specific strategies and techniques for building effective software products that not only improves healthcare delivery but also empowers healing on a whole new level.

❖ ❖ ❖

Chapter 01

The Need for Transformation in Healthcare

The healthcare industry, once seen as a pillar of stability and progress, finds itself at a critical juncture. The traditional model, while achieving remarkable advancements in disease treatment and life expectancy, is buckling under the weight of several converging challenges. This chapter will dissect these challenges, outlining the urgent need for transformation and how software product engineering can be a driving force for positive change.

The Rise of Chronic Disease and Aging Populations

- **The Rising Tide of Chronic Disease:** Chronic conditions like heart disease, diabetes, and cancer are on an alarming rise. These diseases require ongoing management, placing a significant burden on healthcare systems. Traditional models, often geared towards acute care, struggle to effectively manage chronic conditions. The result is rising healthcare costs, increased hospital readmission rates, and a decline in patient quality of life.

- **An Aging Population:** As the global population ages, the demand for healthcare grows, especially among the elderly who are more prone to chronic conditions. Traditional delivery models, often clinic-centric, may not adequately address the needs of an aging population that may require more home-based or remote care solutions.

Challenges in Traditional Healthcare Delivery

- **Cost Escalations:** Healthcare costs are rising at an alarming rate, surpassing the inflation rate in many countries. This places pressure on both national budgets and individuals. The current system is significantly inefficient due to its fragmented nature and administrative inefficiencies, which contribute to increased costs. Simplifying healthcare service provision and increasing efficiency are essential for maintaining affordable healthcare for everyone.

- **Limited Access to Care:** Not everyone has equal access to quality healthcare. Disparities in geography, socioeconomic factors, and a shortage of medical professionals can be major obstacles to seeking treatment. These issues can lead to delayed diagnoses, poorer health outcomes, and increased health inequalities. Solutions are needed to improve access to healthcare, particularly in underserved communities.

- **The Fragmented Patient Journey:** Patients often navigate a complex healthcare system with fragmented care delivery. They may encounter various providers and facilities, with limited communication and information sharing. This fragmented journey can lead to errors, inefficiencies, and frustration for patients.

The Promise of Software in Healthcare Innovation

Software presents a powerful tool to address these challenges and transform the healthcare landscape. By leveraging technology, we can:

- **Develop innovative solutions for chronic disease management:** Software can empower patients to become active participants in their own care through self-monitoring tools, medication reminders, and educational resources.

- **Optimize care delivery for an aging population:** Telehealth solutions and remote patient monitoring can enable healthcare providers to offer more accessible care options to the elderly.

- **Improve efficiency and reduce costs:** Software can streamline administrative processes, automate tasks, and facilitate data-driven decision making, leading to cost savings.

- **Enhance access to care:** Technology can bridge geographic barriers by enabling teleconsultations and remote monitoring. Additionally, software solutions can be designed to address language barriers and cater to various needs.

- **Promote patient-centered care:** Software can empower patients with information, enable them to manage their own health data, and improve communication with healthcare providers.

Conclusion

The healthcare landscape is ripe for transformation. The challenges are real, but the potential for positive change through software product engineering is immense. By harnessing the power of technology, we can create a healthcare system that is more efficient, accessible, and patient-centered, ultimately paving the way for a healthier future for all.

This chapter has laid the groundwork by outlining the urgent need for transformation in healthcare. The following chapters will delve deeper into the intricacies of the healthcare ecosystem and explore how software product engineering principles can be applied to design and build solutions that truly address the challenges faced by healthcare today.

❖ ❖ ❖

Chapter
02

Understanding the Healthcare Ecosystem

The healthcare industry is a complex web of interconnected stakeholders, each playing a vital role in delivering care to patients. In this chapter, we'll navigate this ecosystem, introducing you to the key players and their motivations. Understanding their needs and perspectives is crucial for developing software solutions that effectively address the challenges of healthcare delivery.

Stakeholders in Healthcare

- **The Core Players:**
  - **Patients:** At the heart of the system are the patients, who seek healthcare services for diagnosis, treatment, and prevention of illness. Their needs and expectations are paramount, and software solutions should strive to empower them to become active participants in their own care journey.
  - **Providers:** Healthcare providers include doctors, nurses, therapists, and other professionals who

diagnose and treat patients. Their time is often limited, and software solutions can help them improve efficiency, streamline workflows, and access patient data more easily.

- **Payers:** These entities, such as insurance companies and government agencies, finance a significant portion of healthcare services. They are concerned about cost control and ensuring patients receive necessary care. Healthcare software that improves the quality of care and reduces unnecessary costs can benefit both patients and payers.

- **Regulators:** Government agencies like the FDA (Food and Drug Administration) establish regulations for medical devices and software used in healthcare settings. These regulations ensure safety and efficacy and must be considered when developing healthcare software.

➤ **Beyond the Core:**

- **Pharmaceutical Companies:** While not directly involved in patient care, pharmaceutical companies develop medications and treatments used by providers. Software can facilitate communication and collaboration between these entities to improve medication management and patient outcomes.

- **Medical Device Manufacturers:** These companies develop and manufacture medical devices, some of which may integrate with software solutions. Understanding their products and how they interact with software is crucial for seamless integration and optimal patient care.

- **Healthcare IT Vendors:** These companies provide hardware, software, and services specifically designed for the healthcare industry. Understanding their offerings can inform your software development efforts and ensure compatibility with existing systems.

Navigating the Complexities

The healthcare ecosystem is characterized by a complex interplay of interests and priorities. Here are some key challenges that impact software development in this space:

➤ **Fragmented Systems:** Disparate healthcare providers and facilities often use different IT systems, making data sharing and interoperability difficult. Software solutions should be designed with interoperability in mind to create a more connected healthcare ecosystem.

➤ **Regulatory Requirements:** Navigating the regulatory landscape can be complex and time-consuming. Software developers need to have an in-depth awareness of applicable regulations. This ensures that the solutions for medical devices and software do not violate rules and are compliant and safe for use in healthcare settings.

➤ **Cost Pressures:** All stakeholders face cost pressures, making the adoption of new technology challenging. Software solutions need to demonstrate clear value propositions by improving efficiency, reducing costs, or enhancing the quality of care to secure buy-in.

Healthcare IT Infrastructure and Interoperability

Modern healthcare relies on a strong IT backbone: interconnected systems that manage patient data and workflows. This chapter explores these systems and the critical concept of interoperability.

- ➢ **The Infrastructure:**
  - **Electronic Health Records (EHRs):** Digital hubs for managing a patient's medical history, medications, allergies, etc.
  - **Hospital Information Systems (HIS):** Manage administrative tasks like scheduling and billing.
  - **Other Specialized Systems:** Manage labs, pharmacies, imaging, and public health data.

- ➢ **Why Interoperability Matters:**
  - **Seamless data exchange:** Facilitates smooth communication between systems.
  - **Improved care coordination:** Allows doctors to see a patient's complete medical picture for better decision-making.
  - **Enhanced patient engagement:** Enables patients to access their own health information.
  - **Reduced costs:** Eliminates duplicate tests and streamlines processes.
  - **Improved public health outcomes:** Enables quicker responses to outbreaks.

- **Challenges and Solutions:**
  - **Legacy Systems:** Upgrading older, incompatible systems is crucial.
  - **Standardization:** Universal data formats and communication protocols are needed.
  - **Security and Privacy:** Robust measures are required to ensure data is safe and private.
- **The Future:**
  - **Cloud-Based Solutions:** Offer scalability and security for data management.
  - **Internet of Things (IoT):** Medical devices will generate even more data.
  - **Artificial Intelligence (AI):** Analyzes data for better decision-making and personalized medicine.

By building a connected and interoperable IT infrastructure, healthcare can unlock its full potential to improve patient outcomes and create a more efficient system.

Regulatory Landscape for Software in Healthcare

Developing software for healthcare involves navigating a complex regulatory landscape. Understanding these regulations is essential for ensuring patient safety, data privacy, and successful market approval of your healthcare software solution. This chapter will provide you with a roadmap for navigating this regulatory terrain.

- **Key Regulatory Bodies:**
  - **Food and Drug Administration (FDA):** The FDA regulates medical devices, including some software that qualifies as a medical device based on its intended use and potential risks. The FDA classification process determines the level of regulatory scrutiny required for premarket approval.
  - **Office of the National Coordinator for Health IT (ONC):** The ONC promotes the adoption of health information technology (IT) and sets standards for interoperability, security, and privacy. ONC certification programs ensure that healthcare software meets these standards.
  - **Centers for Medicare & Medicaid Services (CMS):** CMS establishes regulations for healthcare providers participating in Medicare and Medicaid programs. These regulations may impact how software is used for billing, coding, and quality reporting.
- **Core Regulatory Considerations:**
  - **Data Security and Privacy:** The Health Insurance Portability and Accountability Act (HIPAA) safeguards patient privacy and sets security standards for protecting electronic protected health information (ePHI). Your software must comply with HIPAA to ensure the protection of patient data.
  - **Software Classification:** Depending on its intended use and potential risks, your healthcare software may be classified as a medical device by the FDA, requiring

premarket clearance or approval. Understanding the classification process is crucial for navigating the FDA regulatory pathway.

- **Interoperability:** The ONC promotes the adoption of interoperable healthcare IT systems. Your software should be designed to seamlessly exchange data with other healthcare IT systems using standardized formats like HL7 FHIR.

The Regulatory Approval Process

The specific regulatory pathway for your software depends on the FDA classification. Here's a general overview:

- **510(k) Premarket Notification:** For low-to-moderate risk software deemed substantially equivalent to an already FDA-cleared predicate device.
- **De Novo Classification:** For novel, low-to-moderate risk software without a substantially equivalent predicate device.
- **Premarket Approval (PMA):** For high-risk software with significant potential risks to patient safety.

Staying Compliant

Maintaining compliance with evolving regulations is an ongoing process. Here are some best practices:

- **Build a Compliance Culture:** Integrate regulatory considerations into your software development lifecycle from the very beginning.

> **Appoint a Compliance Officer:** Designate someone to stay updated on regulations and ensure that compliance efforts are implemented effectively.

> **Seek Regulatory Expertise:** Consulting with regulatory professionals can help navigate the complexities of the regulatory landscape.

Conclusion

To effectively tackle the many challenges faced by individual players in the healthcare industry as well as the system as a whole, software solutions must be developed with an understanding of their unique requirements and concerns. In this chapter, we elaborate on issues related to healthcare IT infrastructure and interoperability, providing guidelines for building software solutions that facilitate smooth data movement and collaboration within this complex ecosystem.

❖ ❖ ❖

Chapter
03

Software Product Engineering for Healthcare

The traditional software development world and the healthcare domain might seem like separate universes. However, by applying established software product engineering principles with a healthcare-specific lens, we can create impactful solutions that revolutionize patient care. This chapter explores how to bridge this gap and effectively utilize software development methodologies for building healthcare products.

Applying Software Development Methodologies (Agile, Waterfall)

Popular software development methodologies like Agile and Waterfall offer a structured approach to software creation. However, healthcare projects introduce unique challenges that necessitate some adaptations:

➢ **Agile for Adaptability:** The iterative and user-centric nature of Agile methodologies makes them well-suited for healthcare projects. Frequent user feedback allows continuous improvement and ensures the software addresses evolving needs. However, healthcare projects may require longer development cycles due to regulatory considerations and complex integration needs. Agile practices can be adjusted to accommodate these factors through techniques like user story refinement and sprint planning with buffer time for regulatory hurdles.

> **Waterfall for High-Risk Projects:** While Agile is widely used in healthcare software development, the Waterfall methodology might be preferable for certain high-risk projects with strict regulatory requirements. Waterfall's sequential approach, with clearly defined phases and deliverables, can ensure rigorous documentation and strict adherence to regulations. A hybrid approach, blending Agile's flexibility with Waterfall's structure, may also be beneficial depending on the specific project needs.

User-Centered Design for Healthcare Applications

In traditional software development, functionality often takes center stage. In healthcare, however, understanding and addressing user needs is paramount. User-centered design (UCD) emphasizes understanding user needs, behaviors, and pain points through research and testing. When applied to healthcare software:

> **Patient-Centric Design:** Conduct research to understand patients' anxieties, information needs, and technological preferences. Design interfaces that are easy to navigate, accessible for individuals with disabilities, and responsive to diverse cultural and language requirements.

- **Provider-Centric Design:** Conduct interviews and observations with healthcare providers to identify their workflow challenges and information gaps. Design software that streamlines data entry, facilitates communication with patients, and supports evidence-based decision making.

Design Thinking: A Framework for Innovation

Design thinking, a human-centered problem-solving approach, is particularly valuable in healthcare:

- **Empathize:** Conduct research to understand the challenges faced by both patients and providers.
- **Define:** Clearly define the core problems and identify opportunities for software-driven innovation.
- **Ideate:** Brainstorm potential solutions through creative exploration.
- **Prototype:** Develop low-fidelity prototypes for user testing and rapid feedback iteration.
- **Test:** Gather user feedback on prototypes to refine the design and ensure it addresses the identified needs.

Usability and Accessibility: A Priority

Healthcare software must be accessible and user-friendly for all intended users, regardless of their technical expertise or physical limitations. Here are some key considerations:

- **Usability Testing:** Conduct usability testing with a diverse group of users to identify potential usability issues and ensure the interface is intuitive and user-friendly.

➢ **Accessibility Guidelines:** Adhere to accessibility guidelines like WCAG (Web Content Accessibility Guidelines), to ensure the software is usable by individuals with disabilities, including those with visual, auditory, or motor impairments. This promotes inclusivity and allows all patients to benefit from the software.

Conclusion

By adapting established software development methodologies, embracing user-centered design principles, and prioritizing usability and accessibility, we can create healthcare software that is user-friendly, addresses real needs, and fosters positive change in the healthcare delivery system. This concept will be further explored in the following chapters, which will cover practical aspects of healthcare software, including design considerations, development life cycles, and strategies for achieving regulatory compliance.

❖ ❖ ❖

Part 2

Building Software Products for Healthcare: From Concept to Creation

In Part 1, we set the stage by exploring the healthcare landscape and understanding the unique challenges and opportunities in developing software for this field. We explored the intricate ecosystem of stakeholders, the regulatory landscape, and the principles of software product engineering tailored for healthcare.

Now, in Part 2, we roll up our sleeves and embark on the exciting journey of building software products that heal. This section takes a practical, hands-on approach, guiding you through the essential steps of transforming ideas into functional software solutions that can make a real difference in patient care.

We'll begin by delving into the art and science of defining user needs and requirements, emphasizing the importance of understanding the pain points and aspirations of both patients and healthcare providers. We'll explore techniques for conducting user research, prioritizing features, and crafting user stories that capture the essence of desired functionality.

Next, we'll dive into the design phase, where the visual and interactive aspects of your software take shape. We'll discuss information architecture, navigation, and compliance with healthcare regulations, while also emphasizing the importance of accessibility and usability for both patient-facing and clinician-facing applications.

We'll then explore the specific considerations for software development in the medical device domain, highlighting the rigorous software development lifecycle (SDLC) required for ensuring safety and efficacy. We'll discuss risk management, quality control, testing strategies, and the meticulous documentation necessary for regulatory approval.

By the end of Part 2, you will have gained the knowledge and resources needed to guide you through the healthcare software development process, from conceptualization to realization. Additionally, you will learn how to translate user needs into well-designed, functional, and compliant software products that have the potential to revolutionize the healthcare landscape.

❖   ❖   ❖

Chapter

04

Defining User Needs and Requirements

In the quest to build transformative healthcare software, understanding user needs and translating them into clear requirements is paramount. This chapter explores how to identify pain points, conduct user research, and prioritize features to ensure that the software meets the needs of its intended audience.

Identifying Pain Points and Opportunities in Healthcare

The first step is to identify the specific challenges and opportunities within the healthcare landscape. This requires a deep understanding of the current healthcare system and the specific area your software aims to address. Here are some approaches:

- **Stakeholder Interviews:** Conducting interviews with patients, providers, and other stakeholders can provide valuable insights into their frustrations and unmet needs.

- **Industry Research:** Keep your finger on the pulse by analyzing industry trends and reports to spot emerging challenges and opportunities.
- **Competitive Analysis:** Evaluate existing healthcare software solutions to understand their strengths and weaknesses. This will help you identify where your software can stand out.

User Research Techniques for Healthcare Software

Once you've identified potential areas of focus, user research becomes crucial for pinpointing specific user needs. Here are some effective techniques:

- **User Observation:** Observe patients and healthcare professionals in their natural environment to understand their workflows and pain points related to the problem you're trying to solve.
- **Contextual Inquiries:** Engage in in-depth conversations with users to gain a deeper understanding of their context, needs, and frustrations.
- **Surveys and Questionnaires:** Use surveys to gather quantitative data from a larger user base to identify common challenges and priorities.

Prioritizing Features and Functionality Based on User Needs

Not all features are created equal. User research helps prioritize features based on their value to users. Here are some strategies:

- ➤ **User Stories and Use Cases:** Create user stories that capture the needs of different user personas and illustrate how they would interact with the software.
- ➤ **Value Mapping:** Map features based on their perceived value to users and the effort required to develop them, helping to identify priorities.
- ➤ **The MoSCoW Method:** Categorize features as Must-Have (essential), Should-Have (important), Could-Have (nice-to-have), and Won't-Have (can be deferred) based on user needs and project constraints.

Defining User Stories and Acceptance Criteria

User stories bridge the gap between user needs and software development. A well-written user story outlines a specific user persona, their goal, and the desired outcome of interacting with the software. Acceptance criteria define the specific conditions under which a feature is considered complete and successful. Here's what a user story and its corresponding acceptance criteria might look like in a healthcare setting:

- ➤ **User Story:** As a patient with diabetes, I want to be able to track my blood sugar levels and insulin intake in a user-friendly app so I can monitor my condition and make informed decisions about my care.
- ➤ **Acceptance Criteria:**
    - The app allows users to input blood sugar readings and insulin doses.
    - The app displays historical data in charts and graphs.

- Users can set reminders for blood sugar measurements and insulin intake.
- The app integrates with glucose meter devices for data import.

Conclusion

By prioritizing what will best meet user needs and translating these into actionable requirements, you build a foundation where your healthcare system addresses the needs of both patients and providers. Applying these tools ensures that your application solution adds value, enhances usability, and supports a more patient-centered healthcare approach.

The following chapters will delve deeper into the design phase of the software development process, focusing on creating user interfaces that are not only user-friendly but also compliant with healthcare regulations.

❖ ❖ ❖

Chapter

05

Designing User Interfaces for Healthcare Software

The user interface (UI) of your healthcare software is the gateway between users and the underlying functionality. An effective UI is not just aesthetically pleasing, but also intuitive, efficient, and compliant with healthcare regulations. This chapter will guide you through designing user interfaces specifically for healthcare software applications.

Information Architecture and Navigation for Clinical Applications

- **Complexity vs. Ease of Use:** Healthcare data can be complex, but the UI should present it in a clear and concise manner. Organize information logically and categorize features intuitively to minimize user cognitive load on users.

- **Navigation for Different User Types:** Design separate user interfaces or workflows for patients and providers, catering to their specific needs and information access requirements.

> **Consistency and User Mental Models:** Maintain consistency in UI elements (icons, menus, terminology) across the application to avoid user confusion. Leverage established user interface conventions for familiar interactions, reducing the learning curve for users.

Ensuring User Interface Compliance with Healthcare Regulations

> **HIPAA Compliance:** Healthcare software must comply with the Health Insurance Portability and Accountability Act (HIPAA), which safeguards patient privacy. Build UIs that avoid collecting or storing any confidential patient data. Implement robust access controls and secure data transmission protocols.

> **FDA Usability Guidelines:** The FDA publishes usability guidelines for medical devices. Adhere to these guidelines to ensure your UI design facilitates safe and effective use of the software by healthcare providers.

Design Principles for Patient-Facing and Clinician-Facing Applications

> **Patient-Facing Applications:**
> - **Clarity and Accessibility:** Patient-facing UIs should be clear and concise, with easy-to-understand language and visuals. Ensure the interface is accessible for users with visual impairments (consider font size, color contrast) and cater to diverse language needs by offering language selection options.

- **Simple Data Entry and Visualization:** Patients may not be familiar with medical terminology. Design data entry forms with clear instructions and validation to minimize errors. Visualize patient data effectively through charts, graphs, or interactive elements to empower patients to understand their health information.
- **Engaging and Empowering Design:** Use visual aids and clear progress indicators to enhance user engagement. Design features that enable patients to actively participate in their care journey, such as appointment scheduling, medication reminders, and self-monitoring tools.

➤ **Clinician-Facing Applications:**
- **Focus on Efficiency and Workflow:** Design interfaces for clinicians to streamline their workflows and enhance efficiency. Prioritize easy access to patient data, charting tools, and communication features.
- **Decision Support and Clinical Information Integration:** Integrate clinical decision support tools and seamlessly integrate relevant patient data from various sources (e.g., electronic health records) to the UI to support informed decision making by clinicians.
- **Ensuring Data Accuracy and Security:** Clinician interfaces should prioritize data accuracy and security. Implement clear error messages for invalid data entry and enforce user authentication protocols to protect sensitive patient information.

Building Inclusive Care: Accessibility Best Practices for Healthcare Software

In today's digital healthcare landscape, ensuring software accessibility for everyone is not just a best practice—it's a necessity. Accessible healthcare software empowers individuals with disabilities to manage their health independently, fostering a more inclusive and equitable healthcare experience. This chapter delves into key accessibility best practices for healthcare software development.

- **Understanding User Needs:**

    The first step is to understand the diverse needs of users with disabilities. Consider limitations related to:

    - **Vision:** Blindness, low vision, and color blindness.
    - **Hearing:** Deafness and hearing difficulties.
    - **Mobility:** Difficulty using a mouse or keyboard.
    - **Cognition:** Learning disabilities, memory impairments, or difficulty understanding complex language.

- **Designing for Accessibility:**

    - **WCAG Compliance:** Adhering to the Web Content Accessibility Guidelines (WCAG) established by the World Wide Web Consortium (W3C) provides a strong foundation for accessible design. WCAG outlines specific criteria for achieving accessibility across various aspects of software design and development.
    - **User Interface (UI) Design:** Prioritize clean layouts, clear labeling, and intuitive navigation. Use high color

contrast and provide alternative text descriptions for images.

- **Keyboard Accessibility:** Ensure all functionalities are accessible using a keyboard alone, accommodating users who may not be able to use a mouse.
- **Text Alternatives:** Provide alt text descriptions for images and other non-text content to convey information to users who rely on screen readers.
- **Assistive Technology Compatibility:** Ensure your software is compatible with commonly used assistive technologies like screen readers, speech recognition software, and screen magnification tools.

➤ **Testing and User Feedback:**

- **Automated Testing Tools:** Utilize automated tools to identify potential accessibility issues early in the development process.
- **Manual Testing:** Conduct manual testing with users who have disabilities to gain real-world insights and ensure your software addresses their specific needs.
- **Iterative Design:** Incorporate user feedback throughout the development process to continuously improve accessibility.

➤ **Benefits of Accessibility:**

- **Inclusive Care:** Reaches a wider audience, ensuring that everyone has access to the healthcare resources they need.

- **Improved User Experience:** Benefits all users, not just those with disabilities, by creating a more intuitive and user-friendly interface.
- **Enhanced Brand Reputation:** Demonstrates a commitment to inclusivity and social responsibility.
- **Compliance with Regulations:** Adhering to accessibility standards, which are increasingly incorporated into regulations, can prevent legal challenges.

Conclusion

By prioritizing information architecture, user needs, and regulatory compliance, you can design user interfaces that are both user-friendly and compliant with healthcare regulations. An intuitive and engaging UI is crucial for promoting user adoption, ensuring data accuracy, and ultimately, improving patient care outcomes.

The next chapter will delve into the specific considerations for software development in a medical device context, exploring the software development lifecycle and risk management strategies for healthcare software products.

❖ ❖ ❖

Chapter
06

Software Development Lifecycle (SDLC) for Medical Devices

The term "medical device" encompasses a broad range of instruments used for diagnosis, treatment, and monitoring in healthcare. Many modern medical devices rely on software for their effective operation. This chapter will explore the intricacies of developing software specifically for medical devices, emphasizing the software development lifecycle (SDLC) and risk management strategies for ensuring safe and reliable software in this critical domain.

Understanding the Software Development Lifecycle (SDLC) for Medical Devices

Unlike traditional software development, creating software for medical devices adheres to a more rigorous SDLC with additional regulatory considerations. Here are the key phases involved:

> **Requirements Definition:** This phase involves meticulously gathering and documenting user needs, functionalities, and performance specifications for the medical device software. Regulatory requirements and risk management considerations are also integrated at this stage.

- **Design and Development:** During this phase, the software is designed, coded, and undergoes unit testing to ensure that individual components function as intended.
- **Verification and Validation (V&V):** Verification ensures that the software is built according to specifications, while validation confirms that the software meets user needs and performs as intended in a simulated clinical environment.
- **Risk Management:** Throughout the SDLC, a robust risk management program identifies potential software failures and implements mitigation strategies to minimize risks associated with the device.
- **Documentation:** Extensive documentation plays a crucial role in regulatory compliance. Detailed records are maintained for all phases of the SDLC, including design documents, code comments, test plans, and risk assessments.
- **Regulatory Review and Approval:** Once the software development is complete, it undergoes rigorous regulatory review by agencies like the FDA to ensure safety, efficacy, and compliance with relevant standards.

Safeguarding Patient Care: Risk Management and Quality Control in Healthcare Software

Developing healthcare software carries immense responsibility as these applications directly impact patient safety and well-being. Implementing robust risk management and quality control practices throughout the software development life cycle is paramount. This chapter explores strategies to ensure the quality and safety of your healthcare software solution.

➢ **Proactive Risk Management:**

- **Risk Identification:** Systematically identify potential risks throughout the development process, including those related to functionality, security, usability, and data integrity.

- **Risk Assessment:** Evaluate the likelihood and severity of each identified risk, prioritizing them based on their potential impact on patient safety and software functionality.

- **Risk Mitigation:** Develop strategies to mitigate identified risks, which may involve implementing specific design features, conducting rigorous testing, or adopting security best practices.

- **Risk Monitoring:** Continuously monitor and track identified risks throughout the development and post-deployment phases, adapting mitigation strategies as needed.

➢ **Quality Control Measures:**

- **Software Development Life Cycle (SDLC) with Quality Gates:** Implement a structured SDLC with defined quality gates at key stages to ensure specific quality criteria are met before proceeding.

- **Static Code Analysis:** Use static code analysis tools to identify potential coding errors and vulnerabilities early in development.

- **Thorough Testing:** Conduct comprehensive testing, including unit, integration, system, and user acceptance testing. Involve diverse testers to ensure broad coverage.
- **Formal Reviews and Inspections:** Regularly conduct code reviews and inspections by experienced developers to identify potential issues and ensure adherence to coding standards.
- **Ensuring Data Security and Privacy:** Implement encryption, access controls, and regular audits to protect patient data, and ensure adherence to HIPAA regulations.
- **Incident Reporting and Post-Deployment Monitoring:** Set up a system to report and track incidents, analyze root causes, and monitor software performance to quickly address any issues.
- **User Feedback Integration:** Continuously gather user feedback and incorporate it into future updates and improvements.

> **Benefits of a Strong Risk Management and Quality Control Culture:**
- **Improved Patient Safety:** Minimizes risks associated with software malfunctions or vulnerabilities, safeguarding patient well-being.
- **Enhanced Software Quality:** Results in a more reliable and user-friendly product with fewer bugs and issues.

- **Reduced Development Costs:** Proactive risk management and quality control help avoid costly rework and post-deployment fixes.
- **Increased Regulatory Compliance:** Demonstrates a commitment to risk management and quality control, facilitating regulatory approval processes.

Prioritizing risk management and quality control throughout the development process is not just a regulatory requirement but a fundamental principle for ensuring the safety and effectiveness of healthcare software. By adopting a proactive approach, you contribute to a future where healthcare software fosters better patient outcomes and a more efficient and reliable healthcare system.

Ensuring Stability and Traceability: Version Control and Configuration Management for Healthcare Software

Developing and maintaining healthcare software demands meticulous control over changes and a clear understanding of how those changes impact the final product. This chapter explores two essential practices for achieving these goals: Version Control and Configuration Management.

Version Control: Keeping Track of Changes

Version control systems (VCS) are crucial for managing software evolution. In healthcare software development, where even minor changes can have significant consequences, a robust VCS is essential.

- **Benefits of Version Control:**
  - **Change Tracking:** VCS tracks all modifications to the software code, database schema, or development artifacts, allowing developers to revert to previous versions or identify issue origins.
  - **Collaboration:** Facilitates simultaneous work by multiple developers without conflicts, enabling merging changes and maintaining a single source of truth.
  - **Improved Code Quality:** Promotes code review practices, allowing developers to review changes before integration, leading to a higher quality product.
- **Popular Version Control Systems for Healthcare Software:**
  - **Git:** A flexible, distributed VCS with robust branching and collaboration features, ideal for complex healthcare projects.
  - **Subversion (SVN):** A centralized VCS with a simpler interface, suitable for smaller projects but with fewer advanced features than Git.

Configuration Management: Maintaining Consistency

Configuration Management (CM) ensures that all software components (code, libraries, settings) and environments (servers, databases) are consistently configured across development, testing, and deployment stages.

- **Benefits of Configuration Management:**
  - **Reduced Errors:** CM minimizes configuration errors that can lead to software malfunctions, ensuring a consistent and reliable product across all environments.
  - **Improved Reproducibility:** Allows for replicating the exact environment used for development or testing in production, facilitating troubleshooting.
  - **Simplified Deployment:** CM streamlines the deployment process by automating configuration management tasks, ensuring consistent software configurations across all deployment instances.
- **Configuration Management Tools for Healthcare Software:**
  - **Ansible:** Open-source tool for automating configuration with a user-friendly language.
  - **Chef:** Advanced tool for complex software deployments.
- **Integration and Best Practices:**
  - **VCS Integration with CM Tools:** Links version control with configuration management for comprehensive change tracking.
  - **Change Management Processes:** Defines procedures for code review, configuration approval, and impact assessment.

Effective Version Control and Configuration Management are essential for healthcare software development. By implementing these practices, you ensure traceability of changes, maintain consistency across development stages, and ultimately deliver high-quality, reliable software solutions that contribute to improved patient care and a safer healthcare environment.

Conclusion

Developing software for medical devices is a complex and highly regulated process. By adhering to a rigorous SDLC, emphasizing risk management, utilizing appropriate tools and technologies, and complying with regulatory requirements, software engineers can ensure the creation of safe, reliable, and effective software that empowers healthcare professionals to deliver the best possible care to patients.

The next chapter will focus on operationalizing and maintaining healthcare software solutions, including deployment strategies, integration strategies, and addressing key issues in data security and privacy.

> **Case Study: Successful Implementation of Insulin Pump Software**
>
> A leading example of effective software development in medical devices is the insulin pump, where advanced software controls precise insulin delivery for diabetes patients. By adhering to a rigorous SDLC and implementing comprehensive risk management, the software ensured high reliability and patient safety. As a result, the insulin pump has significantly improved the quality of life for thousands of patients, enabling better glucose control and reducing the risk of complications. This case underscores the critical role of well-developed software in enhancing patient outcomes.

❖ ❖ ❖

Part 3

Implementing and Maintaining Healthcare Software: Navigating the Real-World Landscape

In the earlier sections, we established a foundational understanding of the healthcare landscape and explored the process of developing software tailored to meet specific needs within this complex ecosystem. We identified user requirements, designed user-friendly interfaces, and adhered to stringent development standards.

Now, in Part 3, we shift our focus to the equally crucial phases of implementation and maintenance. This section bridges the gap between theory and practice, guiding you through the intricate process of bringing your software solutions into the real world and ensuring their long-term success.

We'll begin by exploring the strategic considerations for deploying healthcare software, encompassing everything from choosing the right deployment model to integrating with existing

Electronic Health Record (EHR) systems. We'll delve into the paramount importance of data security and privacy, highlighting the measures required to safeguard sensitive patient information.

Next, we'll tackle the rigorous validation and verification processes that are essential for ensuring the safety and efficacy of healthcare software. We'll navigate the regulatory landscape, discussing the different approval pathways and the meticulous documentation required to meet stringent standards.

Finally, we'll address the ongoing maintenance and support of healthcare software, emphasizing the need for continuous updates, cybersecurity vigilance, and adaptability to the ever-evolving healthcare environment. We'll explore strategies for managing software upgrades, addressing vulnerabilities, and ensuring that your software solutions remain effective and compliant in the long term.

By the end of Part 3, you'll be well-versed in the practical challenges and best practices associated with implementing and maintaining healthcare software. You'll have the knowledge and tools to navigate the complex regulatory landscape, ensure seamless integration with existing systems, and safeguard sensitive patient data.

With the insights gained from this section, you'll be empowered to not only launch successful healthcare software products but also to sustain their value and impact over time, ultimately contributing to improved patient care and a more efficient healthcare system.

❖ ❖ ❖

Chapter
07

Deployment, Integration, and Interoperability: Bringing Your Healthcare Software to Life

The journey of healthcare software doesn't end with development. This chapter explores the crucial stages of deployment, integration, and ensuring interoperability—key to successfully bringing your software solution into the real world and maximizing its impact within the healthcare ecosystem.

Deployment Strategies for Healthcare Software

➢ **Planning and Environment Setup:** Carefully plan the deployment process, considering server infrastructure, network security, and user access controls. Configure a dedicated testing environment to thoroughly test the software before deploying it to a production environment where patient data resides.

➢ **Deployment Models:** Choose a deployment model that aligns with your software's needs and the healthcare organization's infrastructure. Common options include:

- **On-Premise Deployment:** Software is installed and runs on the healthcare organization's own servers, offering greater control but requiring significant IT infrastructure management.
- **Cloud-Based Deployment:** Software is hosted on a cloud computing platform, providing scalability, flexibility, and reduced maintenance burden. Security and data privacy are crucial considerations in this model.
- **Software as a Service (SaaS):** Software is delivered as a subscription service accessed through the internet, which is cost-effective and eliminates infrastructure management needs, though it offers less customization compared to on-premise deployment.

Integration with Existing Systems

Healthcare institutions often use a complex array of IT systems. To be truly valuable, your software must seamlessly integrate with these systems and exchange data securely.

- ➤ **Standardized Data Formats:** Use standard data formats like Health Level 7 (HL7) and Fast Healthcare Interoperability Resources (FHIR) to facilitate data exchange between your software and existing healthcare IT systems.
- ➤ **Standardized Imaging Formats:** Utilize Digital Imaging and Communications in Medicine (DICOM) standards for handling, storing, and transmitting medical imaging information.

- ➢ **Integration APIs:** Develop Application Programming Interfaces (APIs) to allow other systems to interact with your software and exchange data programmatically.
- ➢ **Data Mapping and Transformation:** Implement processes to ensure data exchanged between your software and other systems is consistent and usable.
- ➢ **Integration with EHR:** Connect different healthcare systems and applications to ensure seamless data sharing and effective use of patient data, improving care coordination, clinical decision-making, and patient outcomes. Middleware solutions can streamline data exchange and accelerate development.
- ➢ **Telehealth Services:** Integrate diagnostic and wearable devices to provide seamless telehealth services for remote patient monitoring and consultations.
- ➢ **Patient Portals:** Incorporate patient portals to allow patients to access their health records and communicate with healthcare providers.
- ➢ **Mobile Integration:** Develop mobile-friendly solutions to ensure data accessibility for both patients and providers on the go.

Ensuring Interoperability

Interoperability enables communication between healthcare systems, facilitating seamless data sharing among hospitals, pharmacies, clinics, and laboratories. It is achieved through the use of data exchange frameworks and interoperability standards, allowing data to be shared across different systems regardless of software or vendor.

- **Interoperability Standards:** Adhere to relevant interoperability standards established by organizations such as HL7 International. FHIR (Fast Healthcare Interoperability Resources) is the most recent standard and uses RESTful APIs to share documents in XML, JSON, or RDF formats, ensuring effective communication with other healthcare IT systems.

- **Testing Interoperability:** Conduct thorough interoperability testing to verify that your software can exchange data accurately and securely with existing healthcare systems within the target environment.

Measures to Meet Interoperability Requirements

Achieving full interoperability in healthcare is a complex process. The following measures can help address interoperability requirements in healthcare software development:

- **Adopt Messaging and Terminology Standards:** Utilize unified semantic terminology and standards for data messaging to ensure full interoperability. Standardizing the content and format of health-related data allows different systems to accurately interpret shared information, such as laboratory tests, medications, or diagnosis details.

- **Assess Current Requirements:** Before implementing interoperability, assess the scenarios in which information will be shared. Determine the types of data exchanged (clinical or non-clinical), the parties involved, and how the information will be used. This assessment will guide the technological needs, such as point-to-point connections or portals, and help identify appropriate standards.

- **Educate Clinicians and Patients:** Provide training to healthcare providers and patients on how to use health tools effectively. Understanding the benefits and potential risks of health data exchange across platforms is essential for ensuring secure and effective data sharing.

- **Improve Healthcare Interoperability with Cloud Providers:** As the volume of health data grows, investing in cloud solutions can help manage the increased storage needs. Cloud providers offer scalable options for storing and accessing health records, improving overall data management.

Post-Deployment Support and Maintenance

The work doesn't end with deployment. Providing ongoing support and maintenance is crucial for ensuring the software's functionality, security, and compliance with evolving regulations.

- **Monitoring and Logging:** Implement comprehensive monitoring and logging systems to track software performance, identify potential issues, and ensure data security.

- **User Support:** Offer robust user support channels to address queries, troubleshoot issues, and provide training on effectively using the software.

➤ **Software Updates and Bug Fixes:** Proactively release software updates to address bugs, enhance functionality, and incorporate new features based on user feedback and evolving healthcare needs.

Conclusion

By carefully planning and executing deployment, integration, and interoperability strategies, you can ensure your healthcare software integrates seamlessly into existing workflows, fosters collaboration across the healthcare ecosystem, and ultimately contributes to improved patient care, fewer medical errors, reduced costs, and more accurate public health data. Remember, successful deployment is just the beginning—ongoing support and maintenance are vital for the long-term success and impact of your healthcare software solution.

The next chapter will delve deeper into the validation, verification, and regulatory approval processes for healthcare software, equipping you with the knowledge to navigate the path to market compliance.

❖ ❖ ❖

Chapter
08

Validation, Verification, and Regulatory Approval

Healthcare software plays a critical role in patient care and diagnosis. To ensure its safety and efficacy, rigorous validation, verification, and regulatory approval processes are essential. This chapter will guide you through these crucial steps, equipping you with the knowledge required to navigate the path to market compliance for your healthcare software solution.

Validation vs. Verification: Understanding the Terminology

Validation and verification are often used interchangeably, but they represent distinct, yet equally important, aspects of healthcare software development.

- **Validation:** Validation confirms that the software meets user needs and performs its intended functions effectively in real-world healthcare settings. This involves activities such as user testing, clinical trials, and usability testing to assess the software's effectiveness, safety, and impact on patient outcomes.

> **Verification:** Verification ensures that the software is built according to its specifications. This involves activities such as unit testing, integration testing, and system testing to confirm that the software performs as intended at the code level and functions correctly within the larger system.

Understanding Software Classification and Regulatory Requirements

Healthcare software encompasses various types, including Electronic Health Records (EHR), Electronic Medical Records (EMR), telemedicine, telehealth, clinical decision support systems, practice management software, health information exchanges (HIE), patient portals, patient mobile apps, pharmacy management, laboratory information management systems (LIMS), and mental health and behavioral health systems. Each of these software types must adhere to regulatory compliance.

> **HIPAA:** HIPAA regulatory compliance is essential for protecting and securing patient health data, serving as the fundamental requirement for various healthcare software.

> **ONC:** ONC certification is critical for healthcare software, ensuring that EHR, EMR, and HIE systems meet stringent standards for functionality, security, and interoperability. Issued by the Office of the National Coordinator for Health Information Technology, this certification validates that these systems support healthcare providers in delivering high-quality care while maintaining patient data privacy and security, facilitating seamless data exchange, and enhancing overall healthcare delivery.

- **FDA:** FDA regulatory compliance is crucial for ensuring the safety and effectiveness of medical device embedded software, telemedicine, telehealth, clinical decision support systems, and pharmacy management software. Compliance involves meeting rigorous standards set by the Food and Drug Administration to ensure these technologies perform reliably and safely in healthcare settings. Specifically, the FDA oversees:

  - **Medical Device Embedded Software:** Ensuring device functionality and patient safety.
  - **Telemedicine and Telehealth:** Securing PHI and ensuring accuracy.
  - **Clinical Decision Support Systems:** Providing accurate, evidence-based recommendations.
  - **Pharmacy Management Software:** Managing medication dispensing safely.

  Overall, FDA regulatory compliance is vital for maintaining the integrity and trustworthiness of these critical healthcare technologies.

- **HITECH:** The Health Information Technology for Economic and Clinical Health (HITECH) regulatory compliance enhances healthcare delivery while safeguarding patient information. HITECH promotes the adoption and meaningful use of health information technology, aiming to improve care quality and patient outcomes. To ensure secure and private communication and data sharing between patients and healthcare providers, various software should adhere to HITECH regulations in the following ways:

- **Practice Management Software:** Efficiently managing administrative tasks while protecting sensitive data.
- **Patient Portals:** Enhancing patient engagement.
- **Personal Health Records:** Providing access to health information.

> **DEA:** The Drug Enforcement Administration (DEA) regulatory compliance is crucial for pharmacy management software, ensuring the secure handling and dispensing of controlled substances. The DEA sets stringent guidelines to prevent misuse and diversion of these substances, including:
>
> - **Pharmacy Management Systems:** Accurate record-keeping.
> - **Wholesalers:** Robust security measures.
> - **Drug Manufacturers:** Real-time tracking of prescriptions.
>
> Compliance with DEA regulations ensures that pharmacies and entities in the ecosystem can effectively manage controlled substances, maintain accurate inventory, and prevent unauthorized access. In essence, DEA compliance is fundamental for the safe, lawful, and efficient operation of pharmacy management software.

> **CLIA:** The Clinical Laboratory Improvement Amendments (CLIA) regulatory compliance is crucial for Laboratory Information Management Systems (LIMS), ensuring that laboratory testing meets high standards of quality and accuracy. CLIA establishes rigorous requirements for laboratory testing to ensure:

- Reliability and Precision of Diagnostic Results: Ensuring that test results are accurate and dependable.
- **Sample Tracking:** Monitoring and managing the status of samples throughout the testing process.
- **Data Analysis:** Accurate interpretation and reporting of test results.

CLIA compliance involves accurate documentation, regular proficiency testing, and maintaining stringent quality control procedures. By meeting CLIA requirements, LIMS contributes to the overall integrity and reliability of laboratory testing, ultimately enhancing patient care and safety.

> **SAMHSA:** The Substance Abuse and Mental Health Services Administration (SAMHSA) regulatory compliance is essential for mental health and behavioral health software, ensuring the confidentiality and security of patient information in substance abuse and mental health treatment. Compliance with SAMHSA regulations require software systems to implement:

- **Robust Security Measures:** Ensuring the protection of sensitive patient data.
- **Privacy of Patient Records:** Safeguarding patient information from unauthorized access.
- **Secure Communication:** Facilitating confidential interactions between patients and healthcare providers.

By adhering to SAMHSA guidelines, these software systems support effective, confidential, and ethical care, promoting better treatment outcomes and maintaining patient trust in the healthcare system.

➢ **IEC 62304:** IEC 62304 compliance is critical for the development and maintenance of medical device software, establishing a framework for the safe design and lifecycle management of such software. This international standard outlines requirements for software development processes, risk management, and maintenance activities to ensure that medical device software functions reliably and safely. Compliance with IEC 62304 involves adhering to best practices in software engineering, including:

- **Thorough Documentation:** Maintaining detailed records of the development and maintenance processes.
- **Rigorous Testing:** Ensuring the software is tested thoroughly to identify and address potential issues.
- **Risk Analysis:** Identifying and mitigating potential hazards to ensure patient safety.

Following IEC 62304 guidelines helps manufacturers ensure that their medical device software meets high safety and quality standards, reducing the risk of software failures that could impact patient health and safety. This compliance is essential for gaining regulatory approval and maintaining the trust of healthcare providers and patients.

➢ **State Licensure:** State licensure is a critical requirement for telehealth and telemedicine services, ensuring that healthcare providers are legally authorized to practice in the state where the patient is located. This licensure guarantees that providers meet specific educational, training, and professional standards set by state medical boards. In telehealth and telemedicine, where care is delivered remotely, compliance with state licensure laws ensures that patients receive care from qualified professionals who adhere to local regulations and standards. This is particularly important for maintaining the quality and legality of medical care and for protecting patient safety and trust. Providers must be mindful of varying state requirements and obtain the necessary licenses to offer their services across state lines, ensuring seamless and compliant healthcare delivery.

Building a Regulatory Compliance Strategy

Developing a robust regulatory compliance strategy is essential for a smooth approval process:

- **Early Engagement with Regulatory Agencies:** Early communication with relevant regulatory bodies can provide valuable guidance on regulatory requirements specific to your software.
- **Risk Management Integration:** Integrate risk management throughout the SDLC, identifying and mitigating potential software failures that could impact patient safety.
- **Quality Management System (QMS):** Implement a QMS to ensure consistent quality and adherence to regulatory requirements throughout the software development process.

Conclusion

Successfully navigating the validation, verification, and regulatory approval processes is essential for bringing your healthcare software to market. By understanding the differences between validation and verification, familiarizing yourself with software classification and regulatory requirements, and implementing a robust compliance strategy, you can pave the way for the safe and effective implementation of your software solution within the healthcare ecosystem.

The next chapter will explore the ongoing maintenance, support, and update strategies for healthcare software, emphasizing the importance of continuous improvement and ensuring long-term value for healthcare providers and patients.

❖ ❖ ❖

Chapter
09

Maintenance, Support, and Continuous Improvement for Healthcare Software

The journey doesn't end after successful deployment and regulatory approval. Continuous improvement, support, and maintenance are necessary to guarantee high levels of performance, security of the software used in the healthcare industry, as well as compliance with new technologies and laws. This chapter explores the strategies for keeping your healthcare software solution at peak performance throughout its lifecycle.

The Importance of Ongoing Maintenance

Healthcare software plays a vital role in patient care and regular maintenance is crucial for several reasons:

- ➤ **Bug Fixes and Security Updates:** Software is never perfect. Regular maintenance allows for addressing bugs and vulnerabilities that may be discovered after deployment. Regular security updates are essential to counter emerging cyber threats and protect sensitive patient data.

- **Performance Optimization:** Over time, software performance can degrade due to increased data volume or usage patterns. Maintenance activities include performance monitoring, optimization, and database management to ensure smooth operation and user experience.

- **Regulatory Compliance:** Healthcare laws are constantly changing. Through regular maintenance, your software will remain compliant with the most recent regulations and standards, safeguarding both patients and your organization against potential legal issues.

Developing a Maintenance and Support Strategy

A well-defined maintenance and support strategy ensures the long-term success of your healthcare software solution. Here are some key elements:

- **Service Level Agreements (SLAs):** Define clear SLAs with your software users (providers, payers, or other concerned parties), outlining response times for addressing bugs, security issues, and technical support requests. This promotes clear expectations and ensures the timely resolution of critical issues.

- **Version Control and Update Management:** Implement a robust version control system to track software updates and ensure a smooth roll-out process. Thorough testing of new versions before deployment minimizes risks associated with introducing unintended issues.

- **User Feedback Mechanisms:** Create platforms where users can provide feedback or report any problems they experience while using the software. Actively requesting user opinions on the software's functionality, ease of use, and potential improvements allows you to address their specific needs, ensuring future enhancements.
- **Knowledge Base and User Training:** Develop a comprehensive knowledge base with user manuals, FAQs, and troubleshooting guides. Provide ongoing user training to ensure healthcare professionals can utilize the software effectively and maximize its benefits.

Continuous Improvement Through User Feedback and Data Analysis

Healthcare software should evolve alongside changes in the healthcare landscape, care delivery, and patient needs. Here are some strategies for continuous improvement:

- **User Feedback Analysis:** Regularly analyze user feedback to identify areas for improvement in functionality, usability, and overall user experience. Prioritize improvements based on user needs and their potential impact on patient care. Regular reviews of feedback can lead to iterative improvements, ensuring the software adapts to user demands.
- **Data Analytics for Informed Decisions:** Healthcare software often generates valuable data. Leverage data analytics to gain insights into software usage patterns, identify potential areas for optimization, and track the

software's impact on patient outcomes.This data-driven approach helps in making informed decisions and targeting improvements effectively.

- **Staying Informed of Regulatory Changes:** Maintain an active awareness of evolving healthcare regulations and industry standards. Adapt your software and processes accordingly to ensure continuous compliance and address any emerging regulatory requirements.

The Role of User Communities in Continuous Improvement

User communities can be a valuable asset for ongoing improvement:

- **User Group Meetings:** Organize user group meetings to foster direct communication between users and the development team. This allows users to share their experiences, suggest improvements, and collaborate on future software development initiatives.They also provide valuable insights into real-world use cases and challenges.

- **Online Forums:** Online forums provide a platform for ongoing user discussions, knowledge sharing, and peer-to-peer support. Actively engage with the user community to gather feedback and address their concerns.Engaging with these communities helps in understanding user needs and fostering a collaborative environment for software enhancement.

Conclusion

By adhering to a comprehensive maintenance and support strategy, embracing continuous improvement through user feedback and data analysis, and creating user communities, you can ensure the longevity of your healthcare software. This ongoing commitment to improvement promotes a culture of patient-centered care and empowers healthcare providers, pharmacies, clearing houses, and payers to deliver the best possible care and services to their patients.

❖ ❖ ❖

Part 4

The Future of Software in Healthcare: A New Era of Possibilities

In the previous sections of this guide, we've explored the foundations of healthcare software product engineering, the intricacies of building effective software solutions, and the steps involved in implementing and maintaining them within the complex healthcare ecosystem. We've covered a vast landscape, from understanding user needs and designing intuitive interfaces to navigating regulatory hurdles and ensuring interoperability.

This section delves into the cutting-edge technologies that are reshaping healthcare software, offering glimpses into a future where artificial intelligence diagnoses diseases, big data unlocks personalized treatments, and virtual care bridges geographical barriers. We will also consider the ethical issues associated with these influential tools as we seek to balance the need for innovation with our obligation to protect patient privacy, ensure algorithmic fairness, and maintain the priceless importance of human connectivity in healthcare.

As we navigate the uncharted waters of healthcare's digital transformation, this section serves as both a compass and a telescope – guiding us through the present landscape while offering a glimpse into the possibilities that lie ahead. Join us as we explore the dawn of a new era in healthcare, where software is not just a tool, but a catalyst for a healthier, more equitable, and more accessible future for all.

❖ ❖ ❖

Chapter 10

Emerging Technologies in Healthcare Software: A Glimpse into the Future

Healthcare software is rapidly evolving, driven by groundbreaking technologies poised to redefine how we deliver and receive care. For CIOs and CTOs in healthcare, understanding these trends is not just about staying ahead of the curve – it's about shaping the future of medicine. This chapter delves into the key emerging technologies that are set to transform the landscape of healthcare software, exploring their applications, potential benefits, and the considerations you need to make as leaders.

Artificial Intelligence (AI) in Healthcare

Artificial Intelligence (AI) is no longer confined to science fiction; it has become an integral component of healthcare software. AI-powered systems are enhancing diagnostics by analyzing medical images with remarkable accuracy, predicting disease risks based on patient data, and even recommending personalized treatment plans.

Applications

- **Clinical Decision Support:** AI-powered tools are transforming how clinicians diagnose and treat diseases. By analyzing vast amounts of patient data, AI algorithms can identify patterns, suggest diagnoses, and recommend treatment plans. These tools provide real-time insights at the point of care, helping clinicians make more informed decisions and improving patient outcomes.

- **Medical Imaging and Diagnostics:** AI is proving invaluable in the field of medical imaging. Machine learning algorithms can analyze scans (X-rays, MRIs, CT scans) with remarkable accuracy, identifying subtle anomalies that might be missed by the human eye. This not only improves the speed and accuracy of diagnoses but also has the potential to reduce the need for invasive procedures like biopsies.

- **Drug Discovery and Development:** The traditional drug discovery process is time-consuming and costly. AI is revolutionizing this process by analyzing molecular structures, predicting drug interactions, and identifying potential drug candidates with unprecedented speed and efficiency. This could lead to the development of new, more effective therapies for a wide range of diseases.

- **Personalized Medicine:** AI can analyze a patient's genetic profile, medical history, and lifestyle data to create personalized treatment plans tailored to their specific needs.

This personalized approach can lead to more effective treatments, fewer side effects, and improved patient outcomes.

- **Challenges and Considerations:** While AI holds immense promise, there are important considerations for CIOs and CTOs. Ensuring the transparency and explainability of AI algorithms is crucial to building trust with clinicians and patients. Addressing potential bias in data and maintaining ethical standards in AI-driven decision-making are also paramount.

Big Data and Analytics

- **Data as a Diagnostic Tool:** Healthcare organizations generate vast amounts of data, from electronic health records to claims data and patient-generated health data from wearables and apps. Big data analytics can mine this data for patterns and trends, revealing insights into disease prevalence, treatment effectiveness, and population health.
- **Predictive Analytics for Prevention:** Machine learning models can analyze patient data to predict hospital readmissions, identify patients at risk of developing chronic conditions, and personalize care plans to prevent or delay disease progression.
- **Operational Efficiency:** Big data can optimize hospital operations, from improving bed management and staffing to predicting patient flow and resource utilization. This can lead to cost savings, reduced wait times, and improved patient satisfaction.

- **Challenges and Considerations:** Ensuring data quality, privacy, and security is paramount when dealing with big data in healthcare. CIOs and CTOs need to develop robust data governance frameworks and ensure compliance with regulations like HIPAA.

Telehealth and Remote Patient Monitoring (RPM)

- **Expanding Access to Care:** Telehealth platforms are breaking down geographic barriers to healthcare, allowing patients to access specialists, obtain second opinions, and receive ongoing care from the comfort of their own homes. This is particularly impactful for rural and underserved populations.

- **Chronic Disease Management:** Remote Patient Monitoring (RPM) empowers patients to manage chronic conditions like diabetes, heart disease, and COPD with wearable devices that track vital signs and symptoms. This data can be transmitted to healthcare providers for real-time monitoring and proactive intervention.

- **Post-Acute Care:** Telehealth and RPM can facilitate virtual check-ups, medication adherence monitoring, and remote assessments of post-operative patients, reducing the need for in-person visits and hospital readmissions.

- **Challenges and Considerations:** Ensuring equitable access to telehealth and RPM, addressing reimbursement issues, and developing user-friendly interfaces for patients are key considerations for CIOs and CTOs.

Internet of Medical Things (IoMT)

- **Connected Medical Devices:** The IoMT is a network of medical devices, wearables, and sensors that collect and exchange data. This includes everything from smart insulin pens that track dosage and timing to implanted cardiac monitors that transmit data to healthcare providers.

- **Smart Hospitals:** IoT sensors can track patient locations, monitor equipment utilization, and optimize energy usage in hospitals, thereby improving efficiency and patient safety.

- **Remote Patient Monitoring:** Wearable devices that track vital signs, activity levels, and medication adherence provide valuable data for clinicians, enabling proactive intervention and personalized care.

- **Challenges and Considerations:** Data security and privacy are major concerns with IoMT devices. Ensuring the security of data transmission, storage, and access is crucial to protecting patient information and maintaining trust. Additionally, interoperability between different IoMT devices and electronic health records is a key challenge that needs to be addressed.

Considerations for CIOs and CTOs

- **Strategic Alignment:** Developing a clear strategy for integrating emerging technologies into the organization's overall goals and clinical priorities is crucial. This involves identifying which technologies align best with the organization's needs and creating a roadmap for implementation.

➤ **Change Management:** Introducing new technologies into healthcare settings requires careful change management. This includes educating staff, providing training, and ensuring that the technology is seamlessly integrated into existing workflows.

➤ **Ethical Considerations:** The use of emerging technologies raises ethical questions around data privacy, algorithm bias, and access to care. CIOs and CTOs must proactively address these concerns and ensure that technology is used ethically and responsibly.

➤ **Partnership and Collaboration:** Partnering with technology vendors, academic institutions, and other stakeholders can help CIOs and CTOs stay ahead of the curve, gain access to cutting-edge research, and implement emerging technologies effectively.

Conclusion

The future of healthcare software is a landscape of continuous innovation. For CIOs and CTOs, embracing these emerging technologies will be essential for improving patient care, driving operational efficiency, and ultimately redefining the future of healthcare.

❖ ❖ ❖

Chapter

11

The Ethical Implications of Healthcare Software: Navigating a Responsible Path

As healthcare software becomes increasingly sophisticated and integrated into patient care, it's imperative to address the ethical challenges that arise alongside these advancements. This chapter examines the ethical implications of healthcare software, emphasizing the importance of responsible development, deployment, and use.

Data Privacy and Security Concerns in Healthcare

Healthcare data is highly sensitive and personal, encompassing information about patients' medical histories, diagnoses, treatments, and genetic predispositions. Protecting this data from unauthorized access, breaches, and misuse is paramount. Healthcare software developers and organizations must adhere to strict data privacy and security standards, such as HIPAA in the United States, to safeguard patient confidentiality and trust.

- ➤ **Access Control:** Implement user authentication and authorization protocols to ensure that only authorized personnel can access the patient information they need.
- ➤ **Data Encryption:** Encrypt data both at rest (on servers) and in transit (between systems) to safeguard against unauthorized access.
- ➤ **Regular Security Audits:** Conduct regular security audits to identify and address potential vulnerabilities in the software and surrounding infrastructure.
- ➤ **Compliance with HIPAA:** Ensure that your software and data management practices adhere to HIPAA regulations to protect patient privacy.
- ➤ **Patient Consent:** Obtain informed consent from patients regarding the collection, use, and sharing of their health data.
- ➤ **Breach Notification:** Establish protocols for promptly notifying affected individuals and authorities in the event of a data breach.

Algorithmic Bias and Fairness in Medical Software

AI and ML algorithms often reflect the biases present in historical data, which can lead to unfair outcomes, such as underdiagnosis or misdiagnosis for certain groups. It's crucial to ensure that healthcare software algorithms are fair, unbiased, and equitable in their decision-making, regardless of a patient's race, gender, ethnicity, or socioeconomic status.

- **Strategies for Mitigation:**
  - **Diverse Datasets:** Training algorithms on diverse and representative datasets to minimize bias.
  - **Transparency:** Making the logic and decision-making processes of algorithms transparent and explainable.
  - **Regular Audits:** Conducting regular audits to identify and rectify any biases that may emerge.
  - **Human Oversight:** Incorporating human oversight into algorithmic decision-making processes.

The Human-in-the-Loop Approach to Healthcare AI

While AI offers tremendous potential in healthcare, it's important to remember that it should augment, not replace, human clinicians. The human-in-the-loop approach emphasizes collaboration between humans and AI systems. Clinicians should remain actively involved in the decision-making process, using AI as a tool to enhance their expertise and judgment. This approach ensures that the final decisions about patient care are made with both clinical expertise and the insights provided by AI.

- **Benefits:**
  - **Enhanced Accuracy:** Combining human judgment with AI analysis can lead to more accurate diagnoses and treatment plans.
  - **Ethical Decision-Making:** Clinicians can consider ethical and social factors that may not be captured by algorithms.

- **Patient Trust:** Patients are more likely to trust decisions made collaboratively by people and AI.
- **Continuous Learning:** The feedback loop between clinicians and AI systems can lead to continuous improvement and refinement of algorithms.

Ethical Considerations for Remote Patient Care

Telehealth and remote patient monitoring offer numerous benefits, but they also raise ethical concerns. Ensuring equitable access to care, maintaining patient privacy in virtual consultations, and addressing the potential for technology-induced isolation are important considerations. It's crucial to develop ethical guidelines and best practices for remote patient care that prioritize patient well-being, confidentiality, and the continuity of care.

➢ **Ethical Guidelines:**
- **Equitable Access:** Ensuring that telehealth services are accessible to all patients, regardless of their location or socioeconomic status.
- **Privacy and Security:** Implementing strict privacy and security measures to protect patient data transmitted during virtual consultations.
- **Patient Autonomy:** Respecting patient autonomy and ensuring that they have the right to choose between in-person and virtual care options.
- **Continuity of Care:** Establishing clear protocols for transferring patient care between virtual and in-person settings.

Conclusion

Navigating the ethical landscape of healthcare software is essential for creating responsible and effective solutions. By prioritizing data privacy and security, addressing algorithmic bias, embracing the human-in-the-loop approach, and establishing ethical guidelines for remote care, we can ensure that technology serves patients fairly and securely. Committing to these ethical practices will help maintain trust, enhance care quality, and support a more equitable healthcare system.

❖ ❖ ❖

Chapter
12

Conclusion: The Road Ahead for Transforming Healthcare - A Call to Action

Throughout this guide, we've journeyed through the dynamic world of healthcare software, exploring its potential to revolutionize how we prevent, diagnose, treat, and manage health conditions. We've witnessed the transformative power of technology, from enhancing patient care through user-centric design to harnessing the power of AI and big data for personalized medicine. We've also examined the ethical dilemmas that come with these advancements, emphasizing the importance of responsible innovation.

The Role of Software Product Engineering in Healthcare Innovation

Software product engineering is at the heart of driving healthcare innovation. It goes beyond coding; it involves understanding the unique needs of patients, clinicians, and healthcare organizations. It's about translating medical knowledge into functional software solutions that improve lives. The future of healthcare is inseparably linked to the creativity, ingenuity, and ethical compass of software product engineers.

The Future of Software-Driven Healthcare Delivery

The road ahead is filled with promises. As technology continues to evolve at an unprecedented pace, healthcare software will become even more integrated into our daily lives. We can anticipate:

- **More Personalized Care:** AI and ML will enable increasingly tailored treatment plans based on individual patient data, leading to better outcomes and fewer adverse events.

- **Enhanced Diagnostics:** AI-powered tools will assist clinicians in making faster, more accurate diagnoses, potentially saving lives.

- **Expanded Access to Care:** Telehealth and remote patient monitoring will bridge geographical barriers, ensuring that quality care reaches even the most remote communities.

- **Data-Driven Decision Making:** Big data analytics will empower healthcare organizations to optimize resource allocation, predict disease outbreaks, and improve population health.

- **Patient Empowerment:** Patients will have greater access to their health data and more control over their healthcare decisions.

A Call to Action for Building a Healthier Tomorrow

The transformation of healthcare is not a spectator sport. It requires the active participation of software product engineers, clinicians, policymakers, patients, and advocates. We must collaborate to:

- **Prioritize User Needs:** Design software solutions that genuinely address the needs and pain points of patients and healthcare providers.

- **Ensure Ethical Development:** Develop AI and ML algorithms that are transparent, fair, and unbiased.

- **Protect Patient Privacy:** Safeguard sensitive health data with robust security measures and adhere to strict privacy regulations.

- **Foster Collaboration:** Break down silos between disciplines and foster collaboration between software engineers, clinicians, and other stakeholders to enhance the effectiveness of healthcare solutions.

- **Advocate for Equity:** Ensure that the benefits of healthcare software are accessible to all, regardless of socioeconomic status or geographical location.

Conclusion

As we stand on the cusp of a new era in healthcare, the potential for positive change is immense. By embracing innovation responsibly, prioritizing patient well-being, and working collaboratively, we can harness the power of software to build a healthier, more equitable, and more accessible healthcare system for generations to come.

Appendix

A. Glossary of Healthcare Terms

This glossary provides definitions for some commonly encountered terms in healthcare software development and implementation:

General Healthcare Terms

- **Clinical Decision Support (CDS):** Systems that provide healthcare professionals with patient-specific recommendations and information to support clinical decision-making at the point of care.

- **Electronic Health Record (EHR):** A digital record of a patient's medical history, including details such as demographics, diagnoses, medications, allergies, immunizations, laboratory results, and radiology reports.

- **Health Insurance Portability and Accountability Act (HIPAA):** A set of federal regulations in the United States that protect the privacy of individually identifiable health information.

- **Interoperability:** The ability of different healthcare information systems to exchange data seamlessly and communicate effectively.

- **Population Health Management:** The practice of managing the health of a defined population by identifying and addressing the needs of the entire group, rather than focusing only on individual patients.

- **Telemedicine:** The use of telecommunications technology to provide healthcare services remotely, such as video consultations or remote patient monitoring.

Software Development and Project Management Terms

- **Acceptance Criteria:** Specific conditions or requirements that a software feature or functionality must meet to be considered complete and successful.

- **Agile Methodology:** An iterative approach to project management that emphasizes flexibility, rapid development cycles, and continuous improvement through user feedback.

- **Application Programming Interface (API):** A set of protocols and tools that allow different software applications to communicate and exchange data with each other.

- **Gantt Chart:** This is an illustrated plan for accomplishing projects that presents information such as the activities involved, their timing, and the relationships between them.

- **Risk Management:** The process of identifying, assessing, and mitigating potential risks that could impact a project's success.

- **Software Development Lifecycle (SDLC):** These are organized steps followed in developing software applications, ranging from planning and designing to coding, testing, development, and maintenance phases.
- **User Story:** A brief description of a software feature from the perspective of the user, outlining the functionality and its value to the user.
- **Usability Testing:** The process of evaluating a software application's ease of use and user experience by observing real users interact with the software.
- **Validation vs. Verification:**
  - **Validation:** Confirms that the software meets user needs and performs its intended function effectively in a real-world healthcare setting.
  - **Verification:** Ensures the software is built according to its specifications and functions as designed at the code level.
- **Work Breakdown Structure (WBS):** A hierarchical breakdown of a project into smaller, more manageable tasks.
- **Software Classification:** The FDA classifies medical devices based on their level of risk to patients, which determines the type of regulatory review required for market clearance.

Additional Notes

- This glossary is not exhaustive and only includes a selection of common terms.

> The specific definitions of some terms may vary depending on the context.
> It is always recommended to consult with relevant regulatory bodies and healthcare professionals for the most up-to-date information.

❖ ❖ ❖

B. Resilient Product Development Framework (RPDF)

Overview

Resilient product development is a framework that extends beyond traditional SDLC or similar processes in the IT industry. It involves unique challenges that can only be learned through experience and helps in achieving a successful software product.

The Resilient Product Development Framework (RPDF) covers the technical aspects of software development in its subsections, known as Architecture and Design Activities. Additionally, it addresses various factors that govern the overall coding and development activities, referred to as the Coding and Development Cycle.

RPDF is a collection of best practices we have identified to address all design issues, ensuring that requirements are managed appropriately and timely. To promote the development of a versatile product CTO's and CIO's can make best use of this chapter to leverage the experience gained in years.

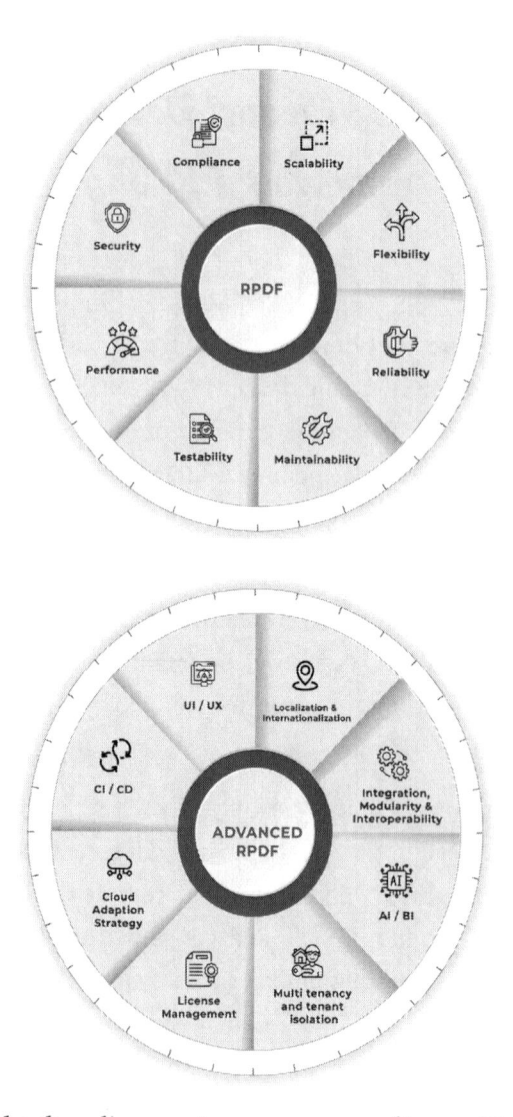

Note: Use the above diagrams to assess your compliance with the RPDF. Fill each block with the % compliance in each dimension.

1. **Flexibility and Adaptability:** Flexibility in product development is about creating a system and process that can adapt to change without significant rework, thereby

improving the system's longevity, maintainability, and ability to meet changing requirements and environments. Design Flexibility can be achieved through loose coupling, high cohesion, and design patterns.

2. **Scalability:** Products should be able to scale up or down easily to handle increased loads without compromising performance or reliability. Scalability is supported by best practices such as Microservices Architecture, Load Balancing, Diverse Caching Strategies, and Data Partitioning.

3. **Reliability:** Ensure that the product operates consistently and performs as expected under various conditions. Most importantly, the service should be accessible and operational with minimal downtime. The reliability of product development depends on Fault Tolerance, Redundancy, Error Handling, Logging, Monitoring, Alerts, and, last but not least, a rollback plan

4. **Performance:** Optimizing the speed and responsiveness of the product is essential for delivering a smooth user experience. Strong performance is supported by messaging and event queues, concurrency and parallelism, retry / reprocessing mechanisms, and, ideally, code profiling.

5. **Security:** Products must prioritize security features to protect against unauthorized access, data breaches, or cyber-attacks. This includes robust authentication mechanisms, encryption, and secure communication protocols. Key considerations from the beginning should include federated Identity and access management, data encryption, input validation, session Management, and API and application security.

6. **Compliance and Standards:** Adhering to industry standards and regulations ensures that products meet legal requirements and best practices. This helps build trust with customers and stakeholders while safeguarding against severe penalties. Product development should involve identifying and understanding applicable regulations, regular audits and assessments, tracking vulnerabilities, and ensuring continuous compliance.
7. **Testability:** Testability ensures that the product can be effectively tested for correctness and reliability. A robust product undergoes extensive testing, categorized into functional and non-functional testing phases. All phases are equally important, including unit, integration, system, and acceptance testing, as well as performance, load, stress, usability, security, compatibility, reliability, and compliance testing.
8. **Maintainability:** Ease of maintaining and updating the product over its lifecycle is a major factor in assessing a product. Key factors that enhance maintainability include real-time centralized logging, app/API gateway, distributed tracing, rate limiting, throttling and documentation
9. **User-Centric Design:** Prioritizing user experience and usability ensures that products are intuitive and easy to use, enhancing user satisfaction and adoption. Keeping the user first, along with conducting segment research, competitive analysis, usability testing, and gathering feedback are key criteria for developing a successful user-centric design.
10. **Localization & Internationalization:** Identify and implement features needed for local and global environment,

to make the software product adaptable and reduce the chances of rejection. This includes formatting dates, numbers, and currencies, acceptable measurement units, supporting multiple languages, maintaining code quality and standards, ensuring legal compliance, and considering cultural factors such as color, religious symbols, icons, and superstitions related to bad luck.

11. **Integrations, Interoperability and Modularity:** Integrating with in-house, third-party, and proprietary applications is crucial for software development. Examples include EHR in healthcare, client data in banking, EDI in e-commerce, and CRM and marketing tools, in manufacturing. Using universally accepted standards in design, communication protocol and integration ensures interoperability.

    A single software application can consist of independent modules, each encapsulating specific functionality. These modules can be developed, tested, and maintained separately easing integration. Communication protocols and standards such as HTTPS, SFTP, MLLP, RPC, REST, SOAP, EDI, HL7 and FHIR facilitate data exchange and maintain interoperability.

12. **Artificial and Business Intelligence (AI / BI):** Artificial intelligence (AI) performs tasks that typically require human intelligence, such as understanding natural language, recognizing patterns, making decisions, and learning from data. In software product development, AI can automate testing and debugging, enhance code quality with automated code reviews, optimize project management with predictive

analytics, improve user experience through personalized recommendations, and speed up development with AI-assisted coding tools. Business Intelligence (BI) involves using data analysis tools and techniques to transform raw data into actionable insights for strategic decision-making. In software product development, BI helps identify market trends and customer needs, guide feature development with data-driven insights, monitor product performance and user engagement, optimize resource allocation and project timelines, and enhance decision-making with real-time data analysis.

13. **Multitenancy with Tenant Isolation:** A multitenant architecture supports multiple tenants securely, ensuring data isolation and privacy. Efficient resource utilization for shared infrastructure can be achieved using a single database with shared schema, shared tables, or row-level isolation. Design patterns include shared database-shared schema, shared database-multiple schemas, and multiple databases-multiple schemas.

14. **License Management:** Market analysis informs the choice of licensing models such as perpetual, subscription, floating, or usage-based. Effective license management involves monitoring usage, detecting anomalies, managing renewals, and ensuring security compliance. Licensing methods should be recommended to clients based on their usage, compliance needs, and cost considerations.

15. **Cloud Adaptation Strategy:**
    a. **SaaS/PaaS/IaaS/Serverless:** Based on the type of application, infrastructure requirements, and user

needs, the cloud adaptation strategy is selected as SaaS, PaaS, IaaS, or serverless.

b. **Hybrid/Private/Public/Gov:** Based on security, compliance, scalability, and control needs, the type of cloud hosting can be chosen as public, private, government, or hybrid.

c. **Containerization/Orchestration/Monitoring:** Use containerization for isolated and consistent environments to enhance scalability and deployment. Opt for Docker for simplicity and wide adoption. Use orchestration with Kubernetes when managing multiple containers to ensure automatic scaling and high availability. Choose Kubernetes for its robust ecosystem and flexibility.

16. **Continuous Integration and Continuous Deployment (CI/CD) Practices:** Implement CI/CD to streamline development, testing, and deployment processes. Use version control systems like Git for efficient collaboration and code management. Automate builds and tests to detect issues early and ensure code quality. Employ tools like Jenkins, GitLab CI, or GitHub Actions for seamless integration and deployment pipelines. Foster a DevOps culture to enhance communication between development and operations teams, promoting agility and continuous improvement. Prioritize security and compliance through automated checks. These practices enable rapid, reliable delivery of features, reducing time-to-market and enhancing product stability and scalability.

❖ ❖ ❖

C: Sample User Stories and Acceptance Criteria User Case

Study: Improving Chronic Care Management with Telehealth and CPT Codes

The Challenge

Dr. Smith runs a busy primary care practice. He has a significant number of patients with chronic conditions like diabetes and heart disease. Managing these patients effectively requires close monitoring, medication adjustments, and preventive care strategies. However, traditional in-person appointments are time-consuming for both Dr. Smith and his patients, often leading to gaps in care and poorer health outcomes.

The Solution

To address these challenges, Dr. Smith implements a telehealth platform for chronic care management (CCM) and leverages CPT codes to receive reimbursement for the services provided. The platform allows him to conduct remote consultations, review patient data collected through wearable devices, and provide ongoing care coordination.

The Benefits

- ➤ **Improved Patient Care:**
  - For patients with long-term illnesses, Dr. Smith's frequent contact through telehealth consultations is highly beneficial.
  - In healthcare, remote monitoring allows doctors to detect and intervene earlier in potential complications.
  - Patients can receive personalized education and self-management support through the platform.

- ➤ **Increased Efficiency for Dr. Smith:**
  - Telehealth appointments enable Dr. Smith to remotely monitor more patients who require regular check-ups, freeing up time for in-person visits with those who have more complex needs.
  - Automated data collection from wearable devices minimizes manual data entry and streamlines care management.
  - The platform facilitates communication and collaboration with care teams and specialists.

- ➤ **Financial Advantages through CPT Codes:**
  - By implementing CCM and maintaining effective documentation of the services provided, Dr. Smith can bill Medicare and other insurance companies using specific CPT codes. These codes allow healthcare providers to be reimbursed for the time and resources invested in chronic care management activities.

- Some examples of relevant CPT codes include:
  - **99490:** 20 minutes of non-face-to-face chronic care management services provided by the clinical staff.
  - **99439:** Add-on code for additional care management services provided in the same month.
  - **99487:** Complex chronic care management (CCCM) services for patients with multiple chronic conditions.

The Results

➤ Dr. Smith has observed a significant improvement in patient engagement and adherence to their treatment plans.

➤ Early identification and intervention through remote monitoring have led to better patient outcomes.

➤ The increased efficiency gained through telehealth has allowed Dr. Smith to see more patients and expand his practice.

➤ Utilizing CPT codes has provided Dr. Smith with a sustainable financial model for delivering chronic care management services.

Conclusion

This case study illustrates the effectiveness of telehealth and CPT codes as valuable tools for healthcare providers managing chronic conditions. By adopting these technologies and billing practices, Dr. Smith has enhanced the quality of patient care while achieving greater efficiency and financial stability in his practice. This approach paves the way for a more sustainable and effective model of chronic care delivery within the healthcare landscape.

❖   ❖   ❖

Case Study: Empowering Diabetes Management with Remote Patient Monitoring and Remote Therapeutic Monitoring

The Challenge

Sarah, a 45-year-old working woman, has Type 2 diabetes. Managing her condition requires consistent blood sugar monitoring, adherence to medication, and regular consultations with her endocrinologist, Dr. Patel. However, frequent in-person appointments disrupt her busy work and family schedule, and traditional finger-prick blood glucose monitoring is both painful and inconvenient. These factors contribute to inconsistent monitoring, making it difficult for Dr. Patel to gain a comprehensive view of Sarah's glucose control.

The Solution

Dr. Patel implements a remote patient monitoring (RPM) program for his diabetic patients. This program utilizes:

- **Remote Blood Glucose Monitoring:** Sarah uses a continuous glucose monitor (CGM) that wirelessly transmits real-time blood sugar data to a secure platform.

- **Remote Therapeutic Monitoring (RTM):** The platform integrates with Sarah's glucometer and medication

dispenser, automatically collecting and transmitting data on medication adherence.
- **Telehealth Platform:** Dr. Patel can access Sarah's real-time glucose data and medication adherence information through a secure telehealth platform. This allows him to conduct virtual consultations and provide personalized feedback and adjustments to her treatment plan.

The Benefits

- **Improved Glycemic Control for Sarah:**
  - The CGM provides continuous blood sugar data, allowing Sarah to identify trends and patterns in her glucose levels.
  - This empowers her to make informed decisions about diet, exercise, and medication use throughout the day.
  - Dr. Patel can remotely monitor Sarah's glucose levels and identify potential problems early on, preventing complications.
- **Enhanced Patient Engagement:**
  - Sarah feels more involved in managing her diabetes with access to real-time data and regular communication with Dr. Patel.
  - The convenience of remote monitoring eliminates the burden of frequent in-person appointments and finger pricks, increasing adherence and convenience.
  - Telehealth consultations provide flexibility and save time for both Sarah and Dr. Patel.

- **Streamlined Care Management for Dr. Patel:**
  - Access to continuous glucose data allows Dr. Patel to proactively manage Sarah's diabetes and personalize her treatment plan more effectively.
  - Automated medication adherence data provides valuable insights into potential issues with medication management.
  - Telehealth appointments allow Dr. Patel to see more patients remotely, improving efficiency and practice scalability.

The Results

- Since implementing RPM and RTM, Sarah has experienced a significant improvement in her glycemic control, with her blood sugar levels consistently within the target range.
- Sarah feels more confident and empowered in managing her diabetes with the support of real-time data and regular communication with Dr. Patel.
- Dr. Patel has observed a positive impact on patient outcomes across his diabetic patient population using this combined approach.
- The program has increased patient satisfaction and improved practice efficiency for Dr. Patel's clinic.

Conclusion

This case study demonstrates the effectiveness of remote patient monitoring and remote therapeutic monitoring in empowering patients with chronic conditions like diabetes to take a more active role in their health management. By leveraging these technologies, Dr. Patel has achieved better glycemic control for his patients while improving overall patient engagement and practice efficiency. As healthcare continues to embrace, such remote monitoring solutions have the potential to transform chronic disease management and significantly improve patient outcomes on a broader scale.

❖ ❖ ❖

Case Study: Enhanced Cardiac Care Through Remote Pacemaker Monitoring for Electro-Physicians Clinic

The Challenge

Electro-Physician's Clinic focuses on cardiac care, managing many patients with implanted pacemakers. Traditionally, monitoring these pacemakers has relied on scheduled in-clinic visits, which often require patients to travel long distances and disrupt their daily schedules. These infrequent check-ups may result in missed data, potentially delaying the detection of any issues with a pacemaker.

The Solution

At Electro-Physicians Clinic, patients with pacemakers are monitored remotely. This system consists of:

- **Implantable Cardiac Monitor (ICM):** An ICM is implanted in patients with implantable cardioverter defibrillators (ICDs) to wirelessly transmit information to a secure remote monitoring platform. The ICM monitors heart rhythm, battery status, and the function of the pacemaker.

- **Secure Monitoring Platform:** The platform allows Electro-Physicians Clinic staff to access real-time and historical data transmitted from patients' ICMs. The platform features alerts and notifications for any abnormal readings or potential device malfunctions.

➢ **Telehealth Integration:** The system integrates with a telehealth platform, enabling cardiologists at Electro-Physicians Clinic to conduct virtual consultations with patients based on the remotely monitored data.

The Benefits

➢ **Improved Patient Care:**
- Remote monitoring provides continuous data on pacemaker function, allowing for early detection of potential problems before they escalate into serious complications.
- Electro-Physicians Clinic can proactively manage patient care by identifying trends and addressing issues remotely.
- Patients benefit from reduced travel burden and disruption to their daily lives, leading to increased satisfaction and adherence to monitoring protocols.

➢ **Enhanced Clinical Efficiency:**
- Clinicians can remotely monitor a larger number of patients, optimizing their time and resources.
- Real-time alerts allow for timely intervention and prevent unnecessary in-clinic visits for patients with normal pacemaker function.
- Telehealth consultations provide a convenient and efficient way to address patient concerns and adjust treatment plans as needed.

- **Reduced Healthcare Costs:**
    - Early detection of pacemaker issues minimizes the risk of complications, potentially reducing hospital readmission rates and associated healthcare costs.
    - Remote monitoring reduces the need for frequent in-clinic visits, leading to cost savings for both patients and the healthcare system.
    - Improved patient engagement in their own care can lead to better long-term health outcomes and lower overall healthcare costs.

The Results

- Since implementing remote pacemaker monitoring, Electro-Physicians Clinic has observed improved health outcomes related to pacemakers among their patients.
- The clinic staff has reported increased efficiency in managing their patient population, thanks to real-time data access and the reduced burden of in-person visits.
- Patients have expressed satisfaction with the convenience and reduced burden associated with remote monitoring.
- The clinic has experienced cost savings due to earlier intervention, reduced hospital readmissions, and optimized resource allocation.

Conclusion

This case study highlights the positive impact of remote monitoring for implantable devices like pacemakers. The Electro-Physicians Clinic showcases how this technology can enhance patient care, improve clinical efficiency, and reduce healthcare costs. As remote monitoring technology continues to evolve, it has the potential to revolutionize cardiac care delivery and empower patients to take a more active role in managing their heart health.

❖ ❖ ❖

Next Page: The Future

Thank you for taking the time to read "The Healing Code"! I hope this book has inspired and empowered you to drive change in the healthcare industry.

As someone who has invested time in reading this book, your feedback is invaluable to me. I'd love to hear your thoughts, suggestions, and ideas on how to further improve healthcare through technology.

If you feel there's something missing or you'd like to delve deeper into a particular topic, please don't hesitate to reach out. I'd be happy to connect with you over a virtual chat or, even better, over a cup of coffee or chai. I believe there's always more to learn and discuss, and I'm eager to continue the conversation.

Let's continue the conversation and work together to shape the future of healthcare technology!

By joining forces, we can create a community that drives innovation, improves patient care, and transforms the healthcare landscape.

You can schedule a meet at: *nilesh@emorphis.com*

❖ ❖ ❖